Trash Picker on Mars

Trash Picker on Mars

Poems by

Gene Twaronite

Kelsay Books

Cover photograph: Courtesy of NASA

Library of Congress Control Number: 2016949343

ISBN 13: 978-1-945752-10-0

Kelsay Books
Aldrich Press
www.kelsaybooks.com

Acknowledgments

The author gratefully acknowledges the editors of the following print and online periodicals, where these poems first appeared:

Black Heart Magazine: "Selfies"
Eternal Haunted Summer: "Four O'clock Light"
Harper's Magazine: "The True Believer" (Letters, Lyric responses
    to the poem "By Chance, Of Course," by Wendell Berry)
New Myths: "Wizards at Heart," "Trash Picker on Mars"
Poetry Porch: "Lizard Light"
Poetry Quarterly: "Fish Bait"
Tucson Weekly: "Weeds"
Turks Head Review: "Writing Small"
Wilderness House Literary Review: "Approaching Lye Brook,"
    "Galaxy Flight to Midnight," "In Praise of False Things,"
    "Holy Ghost on the Window," "On Lost Keys in a Parking
    Lot," "On Sitting Still," "Shades from the Chasm," "The
    Bathers," "The Dilettante," "The Handshake," "The Unmerciful
    Leg," "Tug of War," "Waiting for the Bus"
Work Literary Magazine: "Working Man"

Praise for Gene Twaronite

Written with wit and compassion, Gene Twaronite's amazing poems give readers a whole new view of many ordinary experiences of our culture. Nothing can ever be seen the same way again. A few lost keys "Scattered across the pavement / they lay, like shiny petals / plucked from their flowers" become windows into their imagined former owner's soul. In "Mannequin," Twaronite's compassionate view of what was once a semi-human form now become only "eyeless sockets in an empty face– / all that remain of the life / she once possessed" and manage to suggest the way we are all seen by corporate commercial interests. With metaphors embodied in gritty, graphic images, Twaronite sometimes makes astonishing hairpin turns of meaning in his poems as he does in "Trash Picker on Mars," where this planet seemingly "defrocked of its canals / and green men by Carl Sagan" ends up to pose a chilling potential indeed.

Susan Lang, Faculty Emeritus at Yavapai College and author of the novel *The Sawtooth Complex* as well as a trilogy of novels about a woman homesteading in the southwestern wilderness during the years 1929 to 1941.

Contents

Waiting for the Bus

In Henderson, NV

It's just a hole-in-the-wall convenience store
doubling down as a bus terminal
on the road to the El Dorado.
Beyond a wall of warehouses and power lines
projects the hazy image of Las Vegas
against a screen of blue desert mountains.
It is already ninety and, with still half an hour
to kill, I go inside.
A decrepit office chair announces
the waiting room of damned passengers
forced to sit for eternity wedged
between bookcases of DVD porn
with titles like *Drop Your Drawers*,
Ass Candy and *BodASScious*
and a long showcase stocked like
a museum of the tawdry with marijuana
papers, bongs and pipes of all colors,
detoxifying products like *Urine Luck*
and *Ready Clear*, a Venus de Milo-shaped candle,
dagger paperweights and CO_2 cylinders,
radar detectors, gargoyles topped
with little glass plates to serve up snort,
long knives with silver and gold
handles shaped like cobra hoods,
even a corn cob pipe and bronzed shoe.
Over my head is a rack of *Hustler*, *Playboy*,
Penthouse and others harder still.
There is no escape.
I try to pass the time with the local
entertainment rag laced with lusty
leather-strapped women advertising

cabarets and gentlemen's pleasures.
I put down the paper and clutch my book,
reading it deliberately as if to cleanse
myself of these primal images
with a baptism of pure words.
Just in time the bus comes.
I scan the islands of passengers
scattered among the mostly empty seats:
a tidily-dressed retired couple,
two young women in silver-sequined
running suits, and a gray pony-tailed guy
with frazzled beard and vacant eyes.
Gazing at my fellow voyeurs,
I wonder what vices
and passions they harbor.
Together we travel in darkness
afloat in a wanton sea of desire
that defies my sensibilities
as I delight in being part of it all.

The Handshake

In the market we meet,
soldiers of civility.
I see his arm rise,
fingers unfolded.
We clasp and engage,
hiding behind
our small talk.
Worlds apart, we
might just as well
squeeze rocks.
So much to ask
of a handshake
but it's all we have.
For one more moment
we press and touch
the thin skin
that binds us.
Then silently
we step back
from the other in
ever widening circles
to fortified trenches
we left behind.

The Container Store

A new store in the mall
promises containers
for every purpose.
Shelves upon shelves
of boxes, bins, and baskets,
tinted jars and shiny canisters
to store everything in your life
and then some.
Such a clever concept—
makes you want to buy new stuff
just to fill those hungry containers.

Maybe someday
they will sell
just the right vessel
to store your thoughts
and emotions in safe
and accessible spaces.

For playful thoughts
tanks and bowls to display
like tropical fish
their gay frolics.

For darker notions
sturdy cages
of glass and steel
to hold them fast
while you study
their motions.

Don't worry about losing
important memories
when you have file cases
of fine-grain oak
or mahogany
to store them securely
by subject and date
against dust, mold,
and the ravages of time.

To show off your finest
thoughts and feelings—
that first love perhaps
or the lost cause
you once fought for—
trophy cabinets
in the living room
when company comes.

For troublesome creatures
that gnaw and consume you—
hate, jealousy, and greed—
killing jars
in matching designer sets.

And for all the mournful memories
never to be forgotten
tasteful urns inscribed with verse
perfect for the mantel.

Mannequin

Eyeless sockets in an empty face—
all that remain of the life
she once possessed.

There was a time when she seemed human,
at least to a daydreaming boy
burning with strange thoughts and desires

who could only imagine
from the full-scale model in the window
what the touch of a woman felt like.

Who took her life away and why?
Was it some high-level corporate decision
to remove her eyes, ears, and mouth?

Maybe it was the way she looked—
the way she projected her femininity
at the expense of the clothes she wore.

All that matters now is the latest fashion.
No need to look real.
You're nothing more than a rack.

Let the clothes hang
from your faceless body
like drapes or bolts of cloth.

No reason to get all dolled up—
you don't see crash test dummies
with wigs, red lips, and brown eyes.

No flesh tones for you—
just a glossy white or black finish,
as cold as polished stone.

Selfies

The word burst upon our lexicon with all
the subtlety of a *Playboy* centerfold.
In a snap our clever devices provide
puerile portraits of our daily antics.
Yet only the technology has changed.

Ever since we first scrawled images
on the social walls of caves—
here I am stalking my prey—
have we thrust our portraits
into the popular ether.

Whether it be the self-mocking
image of a Van Gogh or Picasso
looking back at us from the canvas
or a *Portrait of an Artist as a Young Man,*
it is all of the same mold.

We don't need a new word.
It is the same game of fame.
But now all that will remain
of us as we pose triumphantly
in front of the Eiffel Tower
while cuddling our crotches are
shifting images lost in the cloud.

Working Man

He worked a poolside restaurant
called the Marmalade Café.
It was '89, when striking Eastern Airline
machinists stranded me in Orlando.

A middle-aged waiter with thinning hair
and upturned mustache, his big eyes
twinkled with mischievous light.

By noon, he sweated profusely as he served
the lunch-hour traffic, a touch of vexation
on his face, concealed behind his smile.

Could you run this burger through the grill again?
I ordered it well done.
Certainly, sir, he replied with smooth grace
as another customer pointed to her plate.
Can I order anything that doesn't have lettuce?
Ma'am, everything we serve here has a bed of lettuce,
he said, trying to coax a laugh from the grim woman.

Next morning, I asked him how he managed to cope.
He grinned. *Oh, we have our moments, sir.*
Returning his grin, I thanked him for his service.

It's been twenty-six years since that day.
I doubt my server had a union to fight for him,
or whether he would have joined one.
His fight was a quiet one waged behind the counter,
a daily struggle for an honest dollar.

And what of the machinists and their moment in the sun?
Their visceral target was Lorenzo—a noted union buster.
After a long bitter struggle, the strikers triumphed
and brought down a corporate goliath,
while most lost the jobs they had fought over—
a Pyrrhic victory to further fuel the raging beast
at the heart of our labor divide.

You don't start out on one side or the other.
As you earn your daily bread—
by wages, investments, or profit—
a feeling grows and stirs like a fetus within,
until a conviction is born.
It feeds upon what you tell it about labor:
a human activity providing goods and services,
or a social class of persons paid by the hour.

Like any organism, your conviction
reacts to the stimuli of self-interests:
Who will bring you the most benefits,
or who will keep them from you.
You know where your money comes from
and who your people are.
You know who to vote for
and who to trust.

Even now, I see my server
working the lunch crowd with cheerful banter.
And I know full well who butters my bread
and whose side I'm on.

Weeds

You see them growing through the cracks
on every corner. Invading our public spaces,
they survive in spite of us, filling parks and streets
with their unwanted faces. Everyone knows
they don't belong here—
sidewalks are for walking, not sleeping.

Where do they come from? Where will they go?
Not our problem. Just go away. Stop making trouble.
Clean up your act. Get sober. Find a job,
like cultivated folks.

The Unmerciful Leg

In a crowded subway
it protruded into the aisle
like a battered sausage,
while the leg's owner,
her gray curly head
bowed forward,
slumbered on.

Beneath a faded dress
her tattered trousers
teased the eyes
to feast upon
the bruised flesh
of a leg torn up
by too many streets.

I was headed downtown
for the trade center,
where from a magic window
I could soak in the vision
of skyscrapers rising from
the fertile money fields below.

Perhaps the subway woman
was headed there as well
to bask in the warmth
of some deep-carpeted corner
until security came
to whisk her away.

That a woman lay sleeping
with her leg in the aisle
troubled no one but me—
tourist from an empty state
where locals prattle
endlessly of the evils
in crowded spaces.

I tried to resist this
complacency of the common.
I must react with *something*:
sadness, despair, rage—
anything but detachment.
But I fared no better
than my fellow travelers.

As I stared at her,
ground up by a life
incomprehensible,
the stony wheels turned
and ground her once more
into grist for my mill.

As I got off the subway,
she did not take notice
it was the end of the line.
And she would not know
that she lives in my brain,
a clichéd image of what?

The packaged feelings
of feigned emotion?
The impotence of institutions?
The poverty of will?

Or just the failure
of one man's vision?

Frankly, I don't know
what to do with her,
no more than with memories
of the twin-legged towers
that I know should mean
something more
than just a sigh
during a pre-2001 movie.

But for now she and I ride
through the subdural subway,
she and that unmerciful leg,
kicking and screaming
until dementia wipes her clean—
a sleeping woman in a subway car.

My People

Neither kith nor kin, they're always there, moving in and out
of my life like players on a stage. Smoking like a chimney,
they sit next to me at the casino, while I cough and lose my
money. They speak to me on the bus, looking deep into my
eyes as if we were lifelong friends. They preach to me from
the corner, saying I'm going straight to hell, then sing me
a tune about finding Jesus. They weave me a desperate story,
asking for money, or simply stare and nod as I say hello.
Silently, they greet me on the sidewalk while sleeping off
their demons. Wherever I go, there they are—today,
tomorrow, till the end of my days.

As autumn turns to winter, I have come to see them more
clearly. Through the mirror of their frailties and vices, I see
my own reflection staring back at me in a face worn by
the tracks of all who have passed before—an indelible
record of our journey together. They are the people
I carry within. I'd show you their picture if I could.

Trash Picker on Mars

In the dim time before dawn
the woman clamped her metal
fingers over a beer bottle.
Her buckets overflowing
with litter from a dying world,
she sat and stared
at the alien landscape of asphalt.
The stars had all faded
except for the one red light
of Mars still defying the sun.
The woman smiled
at the mythical planet
now defrocked of its canals
and green men by Carl Sagan
and the Legion of Reason.
But still she dreamed.
In her electric cart she glided
over the red-gold deserts
of ancient Barsoom,
past the fairy towers
of Grand Canal
and the monoliths of Helium
where a once great race of Martians
lived, played and died,
filling the canyons
of Valles Marineris
with the excess of their empty lives.
Out of habit she picked up
a fluted green shard, then
laughed and flung it
along with her buckets
into the trash heap of lost Martians.

Through the dark grottoes
of Great Rift Valley she roved
to the shores of Mare Sirenum,
whose salty crust reminded her
of past ruins and distant times
when she could still cry.
For a moment she stared
at the sun, weak and small
as it rose above Olympus Mons,
igniting her in a ruddy glow.
She was the Princess of Mars
and there were still a few
unhatched eggs inside her.
And at the edge
of Candor Chasm
she bared her heart
to the silent, scouring winds.
Then into the dawn
she drove to begin
her new race of Martians.

Galaxy Flight to Midnight

First they fled out of Africa,
seeking new sources of food
or maybe a change of scenery.

Then they fled the ice sheets
and dire wolves that haunted their dreams.
From hunger and drought they fled
over the Bering Strait and beyond.

From religious persecution they fled
to a New World of unbridled freedom.
From war, famine, and disease they fled
to whatever country would take them.

They fled the whips and chains
of Southern plantations to live
in crowded cities of the North,
as others fled the same cities
from immigrant hordes and dark races.

They fled into gated communities
to free themselves from parties
and viewpoints not their own.
They fled into space out of boredom
and because it was the last frontier.

Finally they fled from the earth itself,
in their luxury starship cruisers,
all the way to the center of the galaxy
and a big black hole
that swallowed them up,
every last one.

Better to Own a House

It's my body, you say,
but not if you're a woman.

It's not like property.
There you have real rights—
possession, exclusion,
disposition . . . enjoyment.

With a house, you get to decide
who can enter and who can stay.
With your body, men
have all the keys.

They'll open your vagina
and lock up your womb.
They'll cover your body
with a tent to resist temptation,
then cut your clitoris
to rob you of pleasure.

You can sell a house
but not your body.
For that you need a pimp.
He'll work you till you bleed
and keep all the profit.

Better to own a house
than a body.

Comfort Food

Does it comfort you
that the wine you drink
once flowed through the veins
of a god made man?

Does it comfort you
that your flesh will soon
become bread of life
for a hungry Earth?

Does it comfort you
that your feast of death
will bring virgins
to consummate your rage?

Does it comfort you
that hungers denied
will one day set you
free from all desire?

Does it comfort you
that there is no banquet
for the blessed save
the peace of the grave?

Does it comfort you
that atoms once yours
will live forever
as something not you?

The True Believer

The True Believer is dismayed
by a universe born of chance
and a First Mover betrayed.

But the Skeptic sees instead
the universe of possibilities
that infinite chance has fed.

On Lost Keys in a Parking Lot

Scattered across the pavement
they lay, like shiny petals
plucked from their flowers.

What packrat amassed these
foolish gains only to lose them
here on this lonely sea?

Maybe he just liked the way
they jingled in his pocket
and made him feel important.

Or maybe he was on a quest
to reach the improbable goal
of finding their matching keyholes.

How many doors and locks
did he try till he found
the one true lover that fit?

And when the moment came,
did he just sigh and walk on,
or choose to open it?

Transcendence at the Gym

Almost two months
since I joined the gym.
Already I'm in trouble.
First time I noticed, he was
a slim young man doing
chin-ups next to me,
but I began to have my doubts.

A soft quality to his face—
groomed eyebrows perhaps—
and the way he moved
didn't quite match
his broad shoulders.

In the free weights room,
I tried not to stare
as we worked our bi's
and tri's in unison.

Hard *not* to look,
if ever so discreetly.
His loose-fitting shirt
revealed no obvious breasts,
no child-bearing hips.

Releasing his weights,
he uttered a dainty grunt,
and just like that
he became a she,
at least well on her way.

Later, while curling a barbell,
I caught her catching
a shy glance at me,
curious about the
old man next to her
fighting against time
to maintain that image
of sexual potency
which defined him.
I saw a young man
becoming a woman
or someone in between.

All the while we shape
our bodies at the gym,
we are transforming
into alternate beings.

It's a journey beyond
gender, muscle, and bone,
forging new identities
from the flesh and fire
of former selves
to emerge as ...
whatever.

It doesn't matter.

Tug of War

Often it starts in the bathroom—
a hairbrush out of place
or a pill bottle moved
to a different corner of the cabinet
or a roll of toilet paper
going the *wrong* way.

You go outside and it's worse.
Now the car's parked in a spot
where it's never been before.
The garden hose is not rolled up
the way it should be and all
the lawn chairs have run amok.
Impatiently you reposition the hairbrush
and move the pill bottle back
to the *right* corner of the cabinet,
while you half-seriously contemplate
why anyone in their sane mind
would place the toilet paper that way.

It is a tug of war as old
and wide as the universe,
the same push and pull that
holds our relationships in place
like the earth and sun moving
together in another sunrise.

It is the yin and yang of the earth
and moon in their dance of the tides,
the forces between galaxies
as they rush apart in space
and then come back . . . or not.

With planets and stars whirling about
and the fate of the universe at stake,
I debate my next move.
What if I *don't* return the hairbrush
or pill bottle to their rightful places?
Will the earth fall out of its orbit
or will I?

The Dilettante

He flourishes colors
around his palette
and paints the frame
but not the canvas.

She sniffs the wine,
and savors the vintage
without ever knowing
the pleasure of dregs.

He strums his chords
in perfect rhythm
but does not feel
the heat of their beat.

She enters stage
left, Scene One,
and draws the curtain
before the play's begun.

In Praise of False Things

For those who seek the true, conformity to all things real
is the only path to pursue.

But the false has moments too when the quest for verity fails
and truth is seen anew.

Between the false bottom and the true there may lie more
than we can fathom.

And in our falsehood, we may find ourselves at last
truly understood.

If I must bet my soul on the one true religion, I'll keep
a false one in the hole.

If given to false modesty rather than humility,
perhaps it more becomes me.

If I never follow false trails, how will I ever know
what a true one entails?

And if no hope is mine and true hope never was,
then false hope is fine.

Wizards at Heart

A flash of light bursts
from the wizard's wand,
ancient powers unleashed—
a legerdemain of photons
enchanting us in the darkness
of our deepest longings.
We know the magic is not real
yet we believe it still.

We are all wizards at heart,
conjuring up gods and worlds—
even our own existence—
out of the power of mind.

We hurl ourselves into space,
bending its fabric to fit
the models we construct.
We are tricksters of time
stretching moments to infinity.
Dinosaurs dance on Broadway
while zombies never die.

We foresee our future in heaven
as hosts of our enemies
descend by decree into hells
filled with delicious horrors.

We are each a wholly trinity
of word, thought, and image
endlessly inventing our lives
with new realities.

Modern day magi, we come
bearing gifts for the child within.
We cast our spells against the sun
and tides, commanding them to stop.
And who shall say they won't
when you're a wizard?

Denying the Seal

All Right, Have It Your Way—You Heard a Seal Bark!
—James Thurber

Sitting on the headboard
in plain view, the seal
will not be denied
yet deny it you must.

I heard it, he insists,
but that is only hearsay.
A bark in the dark
does not make a seal.

The only way to make it
real is to turn around,
but that you must never do,
for what if it's there?

Argue long into the night,
but don't turn on the light.
By morning it will be
gone, or so you hope.

Say it never happened.
Blame it on his nerves.
Don't ever concede
he really heard a seal.

And if some night you feel
wet whiskers press
softly against your cheek
with a fishy scent,

just turn over
and go to sleep.
Deny the seal or say
goodbye to sanity.

On Sitting Still

If it's true, as Pascal says,
that all human evil comes
from being unable
to sit still in a room, then
I'd better sit here a while.
Who knows what troubles
might befall the world
from my wanton travels?
OK, I'm sitting—now what?
The writer doesn't leave
me much to go on,
just to stay still.
So talking to myself
or computer games are out.
Can I look out the window
at least? Probably not.
Better close it
and turn off the light.
Damned difficult, this sitting—
I find myself itching
to do something, *anything*,
but how can I when
stuck in this dark room?
There, I've turned on the light—
much better. I can see the clock
now—how slowly it ticks—
at least it gets to move.
The air is getting stuffy,
hard to breathe, but the window
stays shut. I can feel my heart
beating, slower and slower.

Thoughts closing inward,
less chaotic now—bits of chaff
floating in a placid pool.
I feel nothing—no self, no striving,
—all is still and the world is safe.

The Bathers

The wall above my desk
cried out for something—
a seascape perhaps,
full of Neptune's fury.

At last I found it—
the perfect painting
by a Frenchman
named Bouguereau.

Attractively framed
in large format,
it looms over me
as I fish for inspiration.

True, there's not much
sea in my seascape,
just a little patch
of blue on the right,

mostly blocked by two
lovely naked ladies
in the foreground
enjoying the beach.

I could say they're my muses—
in a way that's true—though
the inspiration they offer
is hardly poetic.

No daughters of Zeus
or Mnemosyne, these
are women of earth
whose every curve I adore.

I feel that I know them.
By the wry looks on their
faces, it seems they know
my thoughts as well.

They remind me who I am—
a creature of lusts and dreams,
grounded by the tingle
of flesh and blood.

No More Ground

I will fight for you, wrote the veteran
in retort to my anti-war opinion.
But will you run for me?

Run like a gazelle across the bloody plains
from the beast that will consume you.
Run like a river to the sea
forging a new path to freedom.
Run like a backward clock
to a time before the fight began.

Run from the fight to the finish
to the fight that you didn't start.
Run from the great and glorious war.
Run from the clean war
and the war to end all wars.
Run from the dogs and gods of war.
Run for me, don't stand your ground
till there's no more ground to stand on.

Writing Small

It was one of those
early grades when they
still taught penmanship.
I envied the girl
next to me who
wrote in tiny script,
neat and compact.
I copied her style,
made it my own,
writing letters
ever smaller
as the spaces
between blue lines
grew emptier.

One day my teacher
put her foot down:
I can't read this,
write bigger!

Not wishing to fail
penmanship, I did.
But that girl with her
Lilliputian words
still remained
inscribed on my brain,
leading me to seek
ever more compact
ways of viewing life.
Like the cursive
I copied, small things
seemed more

appealing, be it
a house or a car.
Less surface
to clean and
less to care for.
Economy and
sparseness of form
I preferred
above all else,
extending this
feeling even
to my lovers.
Why not when it was
complete control
I sought in my
dominion of space?

Now I write
in script neither
small nor neat
but in a wild scrawl
that winds across
checks and documents
with a will of its own.
I try to slow it down,
show who's boss,
but it ends up
mangled and disrupted,
like a watch spring
suddenly sprung.
And in the checkout
line I see at last

the phantom ghost
of control mocking
me from the screen
while my artless
swiped signature
dissolves into
cyberspace.

Water Fountain Studies

Standing in the hall,
snatching glimpses

of my students,
I am an intruder

in their territory.
A smile invades

my face, spreading
to kids gathered

at the fountain.
For a moment,

they see only
a thirsty traveler.

Then a silent
alert is sounded,

the vision fades.
We freeze

at the watering hole,
poised for flight.

The class bell rings,
signaling our retreat

back to reality.

Holy Ghost on a Window

A thump from outside invaded
my melancholy this morning.
I looked up in time to see
the banded tail of a cooper's hawk
clutching its limp prize while
taking wing from the patio.

Then I noticed a pale outline
in one of the large windows.
Drawn in whitish film were
wings, head and one clawed foot
clearly visible in stark detail.

I marveled at the fine traceries
of imbrued feathers pressed into glass,
like the silhouettes of lost souls
imprinted on eternity by nuclear blast.
There was even the bill and eye socket
looking inward with vacuous stare.

The upturned wings called to mind
stained glass images of God
the Third Person of the Trinity,
with tiny rays streaking out
from where the impact splattered
its body against the fatal mirror.

I knew it was a mourning dove
and not God that was dead.
But framed by a green juniper,
the shroud in the glass
made a fitting portrait

of all the cemeteries I've known,
with their empty promises
that scatter like feathers
blowing from the patio—
leaving no trace save
a thump that still echoes.

Fish Bait

Time is but the stream I go a-fishing in.
          —Henry David Thoreau

If I could ask the writer one thing
it would be this: what bait did you use?
Was it a simple hook and worm
impaled with your usual deliberation?

Or was it a fly made from a feather
plucked with due reverence
from the wing of a dead neighbor?

Perhaps you preferred a bait more primitive,
crouching like a raccoon next to the stream,
attracting fish to your hand through sheer will.

For sure you would not have used
one of those shiny metal baubles
favored by today's fishing dabblers.

No, yours was the direct approach.
I see you not waiting timidly as the stream
passes by, but diving deep beneath
its rippled surface, meeting the fish head on.

Shades from the Chasm

Gazing down at Bright Angel Trail, I see no angels here—
only shades from the chasm: hikers dutifully descending
into hells of their own creation, then plodding upward again,
as in a Doré Purgatory; naked terraces laid down long ago
like the backbones of ancient sea creatures; swallows
darting across the layers, thoughts too fleet to recall;
splashes of red in the receding scarps of canyon walls—
wounds of a bleeding Earth.

Lizard Light

All that remained
was a wisp
of bones—

beads of vertebrae
arching the spine
behind its skull.

Baring tiny teeth
it gapes with empty
sockets at the sun

shining through the
windows of its
ivory chapel.

Four O'clock Light

In the four o'clock light of a fall afternoon
the realm of reason gives way to wonder.
The vision of old is gone too soon.

Stone lichens read like an ancient rune
of Odin casting my thoughts asunder
in the four o'clock light of a fall afternoon.

Do I dare emerge from my sane cocoon
to mine the ruins of a mythic world under
in the four o'clock light of a fall afternoon?

Is it Loki who tricks my spirit to swoon
and feeds this phantasmagoric hunger?
The vision of old is gone too soon.

I wish to ride in Mani's chariot moon
and wield the mighty hammer of thunder.
The vision of old is gone too soon.

For an instant the solid rock is hewn
as the inner child is freed to wander
in the four o'clock light of a fall afternoon.
The vision of old is gone too soon.

Approaching Lye Brook

A few miles in from the highway
and much closer on the map
is a tiny wilderness known as Lye Brook.

Its name conjures up memories of a time
when farmers cut down these woods
and turned them into ashes,

leaching them and boiling their lye
in big iron pots to make potash
and reap a quick profit from the land.

As a nor'easter brought the sea to Vermont,
I stepped through a door in the morning clouds
into the soft green hills of youth.

Upslope the trail led me
through a familiar forest of ash, maple,
beech and red spruce.

The boundary of the wilderness
lay just over the next ridge
or maybe the next after that.

It did not matter.
To hike toward wilderness
is better than being there.

Eliot Porter portraits of leaves
bleed their colors beneath me
and shoot up into my veins.

With bony fingers, a sapling
clings to the crimson leaves
as if it must not lose them.

These are Robert Frost woods,
lovely, dark and deep—
perhaps deeper than I care to go.

The trail crosses a small ravine
with plunging brook that taunts me
to jump across its turbulence.

Uncertainly I leap.
I am not the same jumper of late,
but I make it, this time.

With adrenaline coursing,
I stride through the woods,
reliving all my connections.

These woods I carry with me—
I could hike here with eyes closed.
I come not for new vistas but to touch again:

the scaly skin of lichens on beech;
the softness of moss on boulders;
the furrowed faces in bark …

a forest of memories from all
my trips through these mountains
on the way to another reality.

I rekindle these images,
clutching them tightly
as tree roots to granite.

And in the sheltering darkness
I see my mother's final journey
as not too different from my own.

Grasping at the fading canvases,
she stowed them away in crevasses
unknown, to feed her heart again.

What adventures she must have relived
until the figments fragmented
and her neurons flashed no more.

I see her walking the dawn streets of childhood,
feeling the touch of flesh and earth until
that last leap into the failing waters.

The clouds thicken and I must return.
The woods grow dimmer
and smell of ashes.

The wildness of Lye Brook
lies just over the next ridge—
but it can wait.

About the Author

A native New Englander, Gene Twaronite now lives in Tucson, Arizona. He is the author of six books, including two juvenile novels and three collections of short stories and humor essays. A strong element of the absurd runs through much of his writing. *Trash Picker on Mars* is his first poetry book.

Made in the USA
San Bernardino, CA
16 August 2016